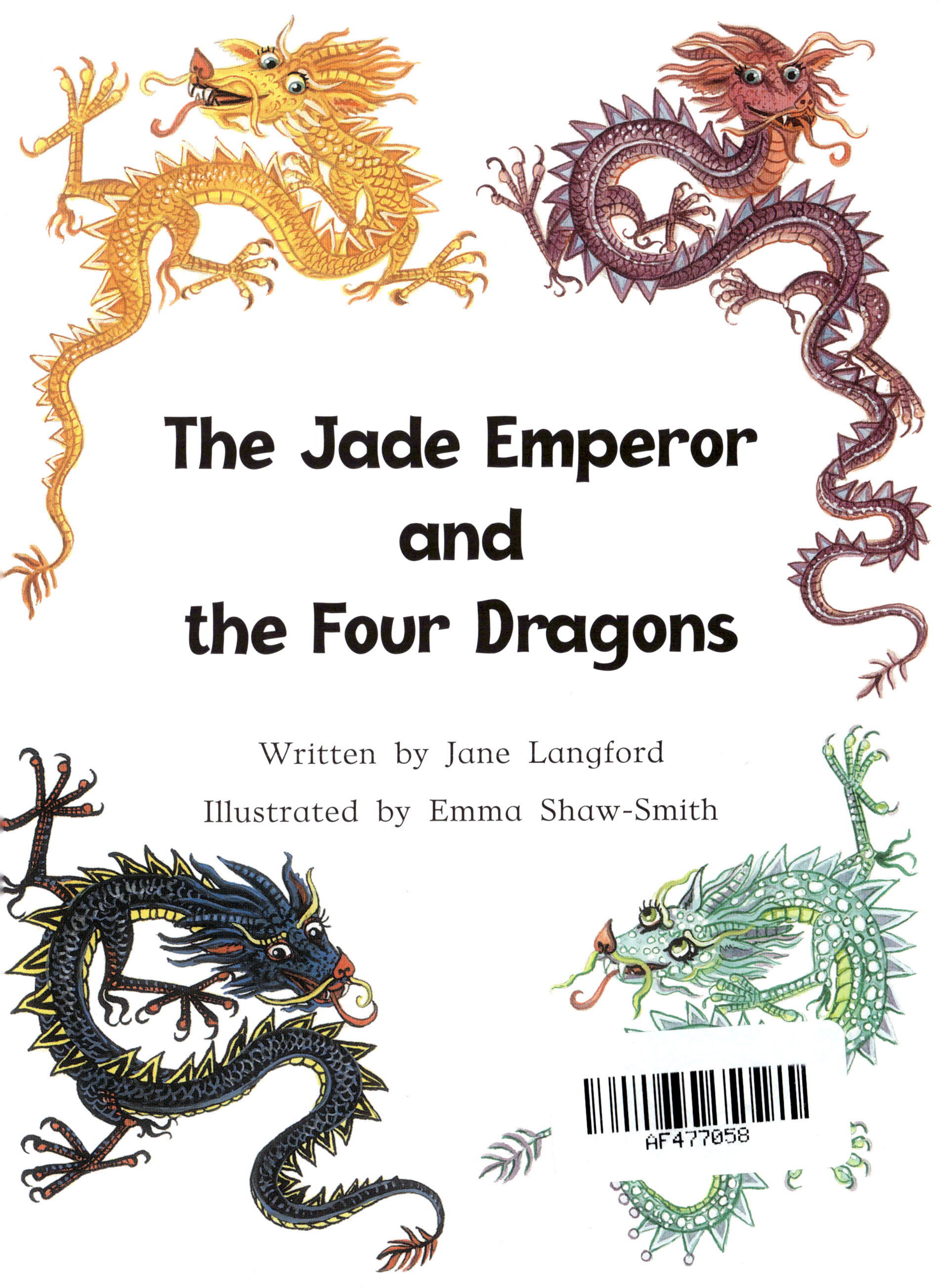

The Jade Emperor
and
the Four Dragons

Written by Jane Langford

Illustrated by Emma Shaw-Smith

The Jade Emperor sat in his palace in the sky. He ruled the sun and the moon, the wind and the rain.

"I want the sun to shine," he ordered. "I want it to shine every day."

So the sun shone and
shone on the land of China.
The earth grew dry and
the fields of rice died.

"We shall starve!" said the people of China.

But the Jade Emperor did not listen.
He yawned and went to sleep.

Four dragons flew over the dry land.
"What has happened?"
asked the Pearl Dragon.

"The Jade Emperor has forgotten
to make it rain," said the Black Dragon.

"This is terrible," murmured
the Long Dragon.

"We must do something," said
the Yellow Dragon.

The four dragons flew to the
Emperor's Palace and woke him up.

"You have forgotten to make it rain,"
complained the Pearl Dragon.

"I haven't forgotten anything!"
said the Emperor crossly. "I don't want
to make it rain."

"But the rice won't grow without the rain,"
said the Black Dragon. "The people of China
will starve."

But the Emperor did not listen. He just
yawned and went back to sleep.

The four dragons flew back over China.

"Help us!" shouted the people of China.

"Please make it rain."

"We cannot make it rain," said the dragons.

"Then we will starve," said the people,
and they wept upon the ground.

Tiny shoots of rice started to grow where
the tears fell, but the sun made them die.

"Perhaps our tears will make the rice
grow," said the dragons.

So the four dragons wept upon the land.
They wept and wept.

"This is no good,"
said the Yellow Dragon.
"We would need to cry
an ocean full of tears
for the rice to grow."

"The ocean!"
shouted the Black Dragon.
"Of course! There is plenty
of water in the ocean."

The four dragons flew
to the ocean.

"How will we carry the water to
the fields?" asked the Yellow Dragon.

"We can scoop it up in the fishermen's
nets," said the Black Dragon.

"But the nets are full of holes," said the
Pearl Dragon. "They will not hold the water."

"They will if we line them with grass,"
said the Black Dragon.

So the dragons lined the nets with grass,
then scooped up some water from the ocean.

The dragons flew across the land. Water
dripped from the nets like rain. Soon the
land was damp and green.

The people of China were happy,
but the Jade Emperor was not.

He woke up and looked out at the
damp green fields.

"Who has been making rain?" he bellowed.

12

"It's not rain," said the people of China. "It is only water from the ocean. The dragons brought it to us."

"The DRAGONS!" bellowed the Jade Emperor. "How dare they water my land!"

The Jade Emperor reached down from his palace in the sky.

He scooped up a mountain and threw it at the dragons. It pinned them to the ground.

"Now let me see you water the ground!" shouted the Emperor.

"We will," said the Black Dragon.
"We will weep until we turn to water.
Then we will rise up through the rocks
and flow down the sides of the mountain."

And that is what they did.

The four dragons turned into water.
They flowed down the mountain
and across the land of China.

Even today, the four great rivers –
the Yellow River, the Black River,
the Pearl River and the Long River –
water the rice fields of China.